DATE DUE			MAR 0 7
GAYLORD			PRINTED IN U.S.A.

I Love to Collage!

Jennifer Lipsey

LARK BOOKS

A Division of Sterling Publishing Co., Inc.
New York

My ok

This book is
dedicated to my
after-school
art students.

Editor
JOE RHATIGAN

Creative Director
CELIA NARANJO

Assistant Editor
ROSE MCLARNEY

Art Assistant
BRADLEY NORRIS

Editorial Assistance
DELORES GOSNELL

Lipsey, Jennifer.
  My very favorite art book: I love to collage! / Jennifer Lipsey. — 1st ed.
      p. cm.
  Includes index.
  ISBN 1-57990-770-9 (hardcover)
  1. Collage—Juvenile literature. I. Title. II. Title: I love to collage!
TT910.L57 2006
702.81'2—dc22

                    2006014280

10 9 8 7 6 5 4 3 2 1

First Edition

Published by Lark Books, A Division of
Sterling Publishing Co., Inc.
387 Park Avenue South, New York, N.Y. 10016

Distributed in Canada by Sterling Publishing,
c/o Canadian Manda Group, 165 Dufferin Street
Toronto, Ontario, Canada M6K 3H6

Distributed in the United Kingdom by GMC Distribution Services,
Castle Place, 166 High Street, Lewes, East Sussex, England BN7 1XU

Distributed in Australia by Capricorn Link (Australia) Pty Ltd.,
P.O. Box 704, Windsor, NSW 2756 Australia

If you have questions or comments about this book, please contact:
Lark Books
67 Broadway
Asheville, NC 28801
(828) 253-0467

Manufactured in China

ISBN 13: 978-1-57990-770-9
ISBN 10: 1-57990-770-9

For information about custom editions, special sales, and premium and corporate purchases, please contact Sterling Special Sales Department at 800-805-5489 or specialsales@sterlingpub.com.

Contents

COLLAGE

IS

COOL!

A collage is a work of art made by gluing different materials to a flat surface.

A collage can be made just from paper.

But it doesn't have to be!

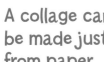

Collage Materials

Here are many things you can use in your collages. What else can you think of?

Papers
- Construction paper
- Tissue paper
- Old art projects
- Junk mail
- Phonebooks
- Junk maps
- Newspaper
- Coloring books
- Greeting cards
- Photographs
- Magazines
- Photocopies
- Wax paper
- Book pages
- Gift-wrapping

Nature
- Dirt
- Leaves
- Shells
- Twigs
- Dried flowers
- Pinecones
- Dried berries
- Snakeskin
- Seeds
- Bark
- Feathers
- Stones

Food
- Uncooked rice
- Uncooked noodles
- Dry beans
- Dry cereal

Trash
- Bubble wrap
- Cardboard
- Keys
- Straws
- Fast food bags
- Plastic lids
- Cardboard tubes
- CDs
- Small toys
- Packing peanuts
- Bottle caps
- Candy wrappers

Other Stuff
- Toothpicks
- Craft sticks
- Cupcake papers
- Game pieces
- Piper cleaners
- Wire
- Fabric
- Buttons
- Ribbon
- Stickers
- Beads
- Cotton balls

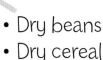

5

Art Supplies

These are the main supplies we'll be working with in this book:

- Paper
- Glue
- Scissors
- Pencils
- Markers

- Crayons
- Colored pencils
- Paint
- Paintbrush
- Plastic cup

When you want to glue something, go around the edges first. Then put a little glue in the middle. Carefully turn the shape over and press it onto your paper.

You can put your collage pieces on top of an old phonebook to apply glue. When a page gets too much glue on it, tear it out and use the one underneath.

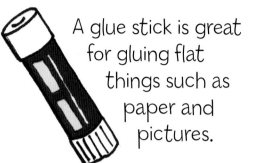

A glue stick is great for gluing flat things such as paper and pictures.

White school glue can be used for almost anything.

Mix white glue with a few drops of water in a cup. This makes it thinner so you can brush it on with a small paintbrush.

Always cover your table with newspaper to keep it clean.

Practice cutting and tearing your paper.

With collage, ANYTHING goes!

You don't have to do all your collages on paper. Try gluing them to:
- Notebook covers
- Jewelry boxes
- Shoeboxes
- Gift boxes
- Tin cans

- Remember to ask permission before collaging.
- Ask an adult if it's okay to use the supplies you find.
- An adult can also help you make copies of photographs or other papers that you want to use.

Try painting or finger painting sheets of paper first. Let them dry and then collage them.

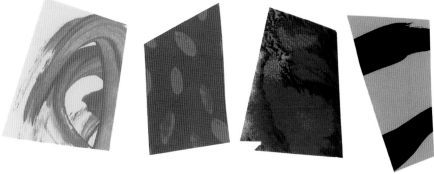

Practice with different colors and patterns.

Torn Animals

It's easy and fun to make animals from torn paper. Decide what kind of animal you want to collage or make one up as you go.

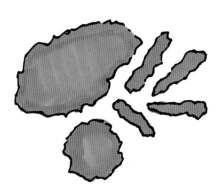

1. Tear a body, head, and legs from a piece of paper. Draw the shapes first if you want.

2. Arrange the pieces on a sheet of paper.

3. Tear out eyes, a nose, a tail, ears, spots, and whatever else your animal needs.

4. Try out the new parts. Glue your pieces to the collage when you're happy with how it looks.

Supplies

- Colored paper
- Markers (optional)
- Glue

What other
animals can
you think of?

Use a marker to
draw details
such as whiskers.

Tasty Treats

Paint your own flavors to make an ice-creamy collage that never melts!

1. Paint paper the colors of different ice cream flavors. When the paint is dry, draw and cut out circles to make scoops.

2. Glue down the top scoop first. Glue the next scoop down so it overlaps the first one. Keep gluing overlapping scoops until you have as many as you want.

3. Cut out a paper bowl for your ice cream. Glue it down so it overlaps the bottom scoops.

Make chocolate syrup glue!

1. Ask a parent for permission before doing this!

2. Take the top off a small bottle of glue and pour some black paint inside.

3. Stir it with a craft stick or an old paintbrush.

4. Put the cap back on and squirt out chocolate syrup.

Supplies

- Paper
- Paint
- Paintbrush
- Pencil
- Scissors
- Glue
- Black paint
- Craft stick or old paintbrush

Try adding sprinkles and chocolate chunks!

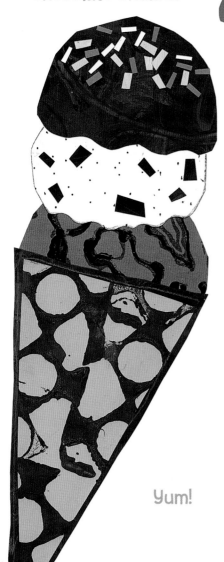

Yum!

Collage a cherry on top.

Don't forget the chocolate syrup. (Syrup glue needs to dry overnight.)

Add a spoon.

Decorate your bowl.

Create a Face

Use magazine pictures to make fantastically funny faces!

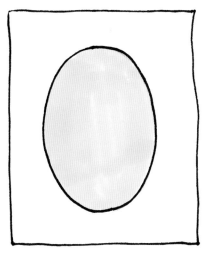

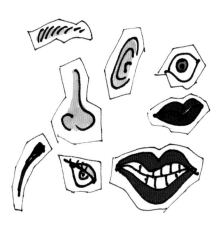

1. Cut an oval out of colored paper. Glue it onto a bigger piece of paper.

2. Find big faces in magazines. Cut out eyes, noses, ears, lips, hair, and anything else you want.

3. Try out different faces with the cut out parts. Glue down the ones you like the best.

Make your faces as silly as you want!

4. Add hair, a mustache, a neck, or anything else you can think of.

Supplies
- Colored paper
- Scissors
- Glue
- Old magazines

Try cutting out a whole face. Put different eyes and noses on it. How funny is that?

Add a body if you want.

How about a veggie head?

Try using photos of your friends and family.

Sand & Sails

Collage your very own sailboat!

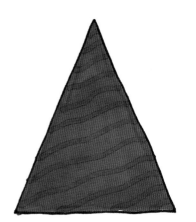

1. Cut out a large triangle.

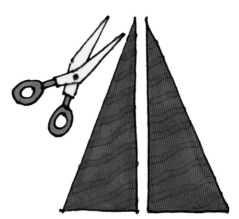

2. Cut it in half. These will be the sails.

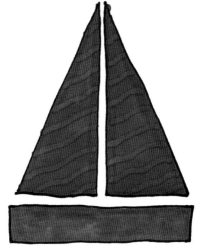

3. Cut out a long rectangle for the boat.

4. Glue the sailboat pieces to your background paper.

Cut out some wavy water. Glue it down overlapping the bottom of the boat. Add a triangle flag.

Supplies

- Colored or painted paper
- Scissors
- Glue

14

Collage Cards

Create a homemade card for someone special.

You can use everything you learn in this book to make cool cards.

What kind of card will you make? A birthday card? A Valentine's Day card?

1. Fold a piece of paper in half. Decorate the front side. Add a special message.

2. Add your favorite collage materials. Try a border.

3. Decorate the inside of the card, too. Write a note. Sign your name.

Recycle holiday cards by using them in a collage.

Wrapping paper is also handy for holiday collages.

Try using real sticks for snowman arms.

Happy

Christmas

Make colorful collage paper.

1. Cover white paper with overlapping pieces of colored tissue paper.

2. Glue them on and let dry.

3. Use shapes cut from your paper for a bright collage.

Use a photograph of yourself to create a collage your mom or someone special will love.

Happy Mother's Day!

Thanks for growing me Mom!

CoolCats

Collage your own cat.

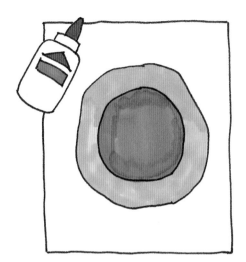

1. Cut out a large circle. Glue it to your background paper. Cut out a smaller circle and glue it on top of your big circle.

2. For ears, cut a small circle in half. Glue the ears on the head.

3. Cut out face parts such as eyes, whiskers, a nose, and a mouth.

Try adding a body, paws, or a tail.

4. Play with the arrangement of the face parts. Glue them down.

Supplies
- Colored paper
- Scissors
- Glue
- Paint (optional)
- Paintbrush (optional)

Collage leaf shapes to put your tiger in the jungle.

Paint black stripes on orange paper to make a tiger design. Let it dry. Cut out your tiger collage.

Finger print spots to make leopard paper. Let it dry. Cut out your leopard collage.

A large rectangle looks like a wall for the cat to peek over.

It's easy to make this curious cat.

Garbage Art

Free art supplies are easy to find.
Recycle trash into awesome art!

How about
a cork bird?

Look around
your house for
things no one
else is using.
How can you
use them?

Supplies

- Trash collage pieces
  (See page 5.)
- Paper
- Scissors
- Glue

Straws, lids, wrappers, and
bags can make cool collages.

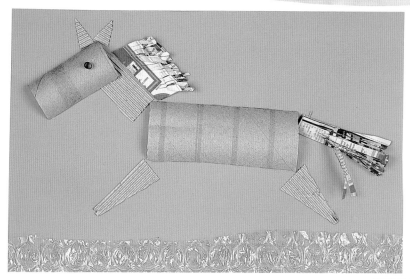

Cardboard tubes, newspaper, and bubble wrap make a fast horse.

Lay out all of your found supplies. Play around with them. Do you see a crazy creature? A funny face?

What kind of garbage art can you think of?

FREE Art

Use old wrapping paper, packing peanuts, and cotton balls to make a silly Santa.

21

Circle Birds

Cut out circles to collage some fine, feathery friends!

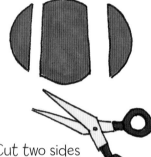

1. Draw two big circles and one small circle. Trace the circle shapes if you want. Cut them out.

2. First, glue the small circle to the background paper. Glue a big circle on so it overlaps the small one. This is the body and head.

3. Cut two sides off the other big circle. These will be the wings.

4. Glue the wings to the body.

5. Add a triangle beak. Cut out legs. How tall is your bird?

Supplies

- Colored or painted paper
- Pencil
- Round objects to trace (optional)
- Background paper
- Scissors
- Glue

Can you make a flying bird?

Collage a background
for your birds.

How about some baby birds?

Add details with markers.

Nature Art

Collect materials from nature to make terrific collages!

Go for a nature walk and take along small plastic bags. Fill them with things from nature to use in your art. How about sand, dirt, sticks, leaves, bark, shells, feathers, snakeskins, and acorns?

Cool feather flower!

Paint your background first.

Supplies

- Collage materials from nature (See page 5.)
- Paint (optional)
- Paper or cardboard
- Glue

You will find different things in nature depending on where you live.

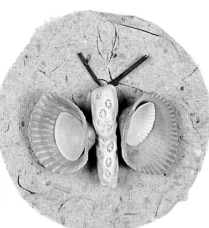

How about a shell butterfly?

How about a stick person?

Try sprinkling sand on wet glue. Tap off what doesn't stick.

Cool bark castle!

Picture This

Try collaging different frames on your photographs for a very cool look!

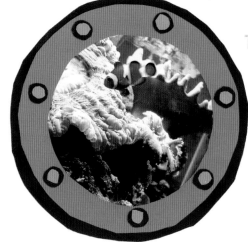

Cut out a wacky shape. Tear a hole in the middle and glue it on top of your photo. Cool!

Make a picture window!

1. Cut out a piece of paper that's a little bigger than your photo. Glue your photo on top of the paper.

2. Cut out two skinny strips of paper and glue them on top of the photo so they cross in the middle.

Turn a picture of an aquarium into a submarine window under the sea.

What other windows can you think of? A truck? Spaceship? Train?

Want to be on TV? Now you can!

1. Draw and cut out a TV shape.

2. Fold the shape in half. Cut out the opening, starting from the fold.

3. Unfold the shape and glue it on top of your photo. Add details. Congratulations! You are a star!

Make a giant face peeking into a little room.

1. Collage a room scene.

2. Cut a hole in the wall for the window.

3. Cut small strips of paper. Glue them around the window.

4. Glue the window opening on top of a face picture. Wow!

Mix it Up

Use bottle caps and anything else you can find to make awesome collages!

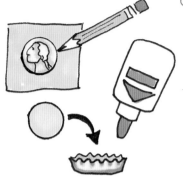

1. Trace a quarter onto paper. Cut the shape out and glue it inside a bottle cap.

2. Look at your collage supplies. What can you make from them? A head? A sun? A flower? A bird?

3. Cut out all of the pieces you will need for your picture.

4. Glue down all the collage pieces. Nice work!

Add details such as beads, feathers, yarn, beans, and anything else you can think of!

Supplies

- Quarter
- Paper
- Pencil
- Scissors
- Glue
- Bottle caps
- Other collage supplies

Cool dump truck!

Look for collage
supplies around your
home like cardboard,
beans, rubber bands,
and newspaper.

If you want your
picture to have an
interesting background,
glue it down first.

Try a tissue paper sunset.

Wacky Wire

Add pizzazz to your collages with wire!

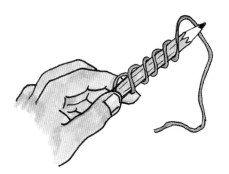 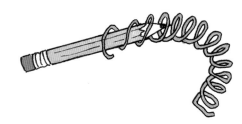

1. Hold one end of some wire or a pipe cleaner on a pencil. Wrap the wire around and around the pencil.

2. Slide the curly wire off the pencil.

3. Make different sizes of curlys by using different tools. Try a skinny paintbrush or a fat marker.

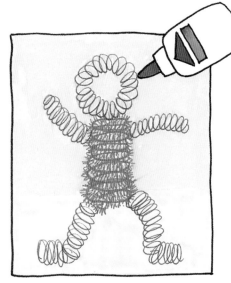

Remember to glue your paper pieces to your background first, and then the wires. Hold the wire on the paper for a minute or two while the glue dries.

4. Make your curly wires into a collage.

Supplies

- Wire or pipe cleaners
- Pencil, paintbrush, or marker
- Paper
- Glue
- Collage supplies

Trace a plate to make a circle-shaped collage.

Add beads.

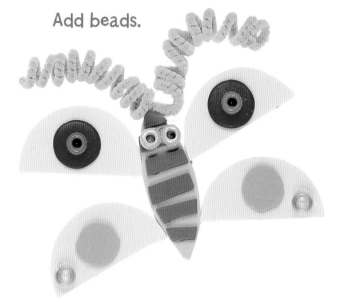

Try twisting wire to make people.

Nice hat!

Twist ties make this girl's eyes.
Thick wire forms the body.

Weave It!

Did you know you could weave a collage?
Ask an adult for help if you need it.

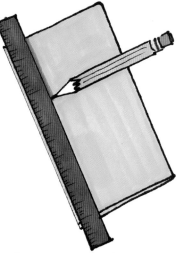

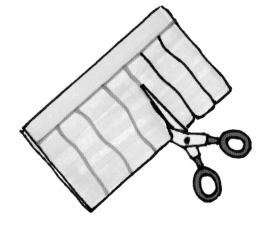

1. Fold a piece of colored paper in half. Draw a line about 1 inch from the edge. This is your guideline.

2. Keep the paper folded. Draw six lines from the guideline to the fold. It's good if the lines are a little wavy.

3. Cut along the lines from the folded edge to the guideline. Don't cut over the guideline. Unfold the paper. This piece is called the **warp**.

4. Cut narrow strips from a different color paper. These are called the **weft**. Weave the first strip **over** one piece of the warp and under, over one and under, across the warp.

Start the next row **under** the warp. Keep weaving until all the warps are full.

When done, pack the weft strips close together. Glue the ends down on both sides.

Supplies

- Colored paper
- Pencil
- Ruler
- Scissors
- Glue

Try weaving magazine pictures together.

Cut a shape out of a piece of paper. Glue the leftover piece on top of your weaving.

Stitch It

Add stitched details to make your collage extra special! Stitching works best with stiff paper.

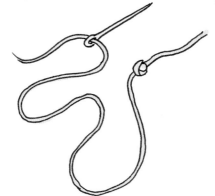

1. Lay a piece of cardboard behind your collage. Use a large needle to poke holes in your collage where you want stitches. (Draw them with a pencil first, if you want.)

2. Tie a knot at one end of the string. Have an adult help you thread the other end through the needle.

3. Start from the back of your collage. Push the needle through the first hole. Keep pulling until the knot stops you. Then, from the front, push the needle through the second hole.

4. Keep stitching up and down through the holes.

Make sure your very last stitch comes out of the backside of the collage. Tape down your string next to the last hole. Cut off any extra string.

Supplies
- **Your collage**
- **Cardboard**
- **Pencil (optional)**
- **String or embroidery floss**
- **Large needle**
- **Scissors**
- **Tape**

This kitty is collaged felt. Stitched whiskers make a cool cat!

Try stitching a shape such as a heart.

This makes a nice card.

Stitches help put the buzz in this bee.

Folded Fun!

Shapes that look the same on both sides
are symmetrical. Try using them in a collage!

1. Fold a piece of paper in half.
   Draw half of something on it.

2. Cut out the shape
   starting at the
   folded edge.

3. You can cut some
   small pieces out of the
   fold, if you want.

Cut other
collage pieces
to add to your
picture.

4. Now glue your favorite folded
   cut-outs to colored paper or a
   collaged background.

Supplies

- Colored or
  painted paper
- Pencil
- Scissors
- Glue
- Collage supplies
- Colored pencils or
  markers (optional)

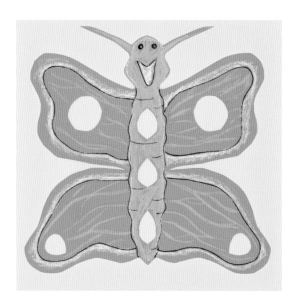

Add more
details with
colored pencils
or markers.

Fold and cut birds, bugs,
hearts, airplanes, monsters,
masks, stars, trees, or
flowers.

What else can you think of?

Try to use more than
one symmetrical shape
in a collage.

How about a giant alien?

Window Wax

Use wax paper to make amazing art for your windows.

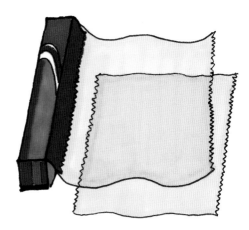

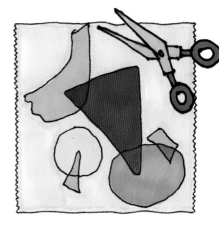

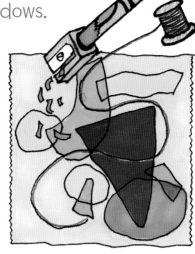

1. Tear two pieces of wax paper off the roll.

2. Cut or tear colored tissue paper into shapes. Arrange the pieces in a design on one piece of wax paper. Let some of the pieces overlap.

3. Try adding some colored thread and crayon shavings to your design. Use a pencil sharpener to make crayon shavings.

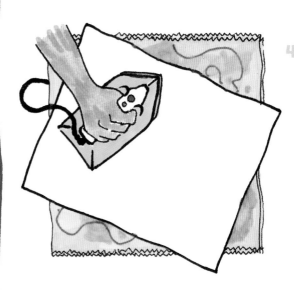

4. Carefully lay the second piece of wax paper over your design. Cover it with plain paper and have an adult iron it. The heat will melt the wax papers together.

Supplies

- Wax paper
- Colored tissue paper
- Scissors
- Colored thread (optional)
- Old crayons (optional)
- Pencil sharperner (optional)
- Paper
- Iron
- Tape

Tape your see-through picture to a window. Wow!

Rip & Stick

It's fun to fill in shapes with ripped paper pieces!

1. Draw a simple shape such as an animal on a piece of paper.

2. Rip lots of small pieces of paper or tissue paper. (Paint the paper first if you want a special color or design.)

3. Glue on the ripped paper pieces to fill in the shape. It's okay to let the pieces overlap.

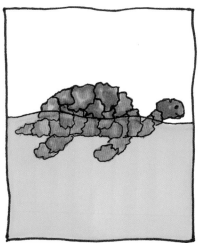

4. Cut out more pieces to add details to your collage.

Overlapping tissue paper looks like water.

Supplies

- Pencil
- Colored or painted paper
- Tissue paper (optional)
- Glue
- Scissors (optional)

Watch out for that dragon!

Cut lots of triangles
to make spikes.

This turtle stays cool in
the water.

How about a collaged
dragonfly?

Glue down some tissue-paper
plants before gluing down the
tissue-paper water.

Furry Folks

You can make funny furry characters with cut-out pictures from magazines

1. Look through old magazines and cut out pictures of animal heads and human bodies. Cut out human eyes, too.

2. Try out different heads on the bodies. When you find a combination you like, glue it all to a piece of paper.

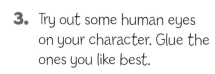

3. Try out some human eyes on your character. Glue the ones you like best.

"Hello there, Mr. Schnauzer."

Supplies
- Old magazines
- Scissors
- Paper
- Glue

42

It's Astrocat!

Collage a
background.

"Paging Dr. Dog."

Professor Bear

43

Glowing Glass

People have been making stained glass for many hundreds of years. You can make your own collage stained glass windows.

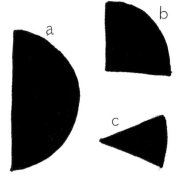

1. Cut colored tissue paper into squares smaller than the palm of your hand.

2. Draw a large circle on a big piece of black paper. (Try tracing a dinner plate.) Cut it out.

3. Fold the circle shape in half (a). Then, fold it in half again (b). Then, fold it one more time (c).

4. Cut off the point. Cut out different-sized shapes along the folds. Leave some black between the shapes. Do not cut the curved edge.

5. Open the circle. On one side, glue tissue paper squares over all the cut out shapes. Let the colors overlap. The other side will be the front.

Supplies

- Brightly colored tissue paper
- Scissors
- Pencil
- Black construction paper
- Dinner plate (optional)
- Glue

Glue more tissue paper over any places you missed.

Hang your stained glass in a window to see it glow.

It's beautiful!

45

Recycle It

It's fun to use your leftover pieces to make something new!

Keep your collage scraps in a special box or bag and recycle them.

1. Start by gluing down your biggest pieces.
2. Next, glue down your medium-sized pieces.
3. Glue the very small pieces last.

Look at the shapes of your scraps. What do you see?

Supplies

- Collage scraps
- Glue
- Paper

WiSH.

47

Do you recognize any of the scraps in this collage?
Which other collages in this book did they come from?

Acknowledgments

I hope this book will be a help to folks that support art for kids. Mostly though, I hope it will inspire kids to explore and create their own unique visual expressions.

I would like to thank Joe, Celia, Rose, and Bradley at Lark Books for their hard work and special attention to detail.

I am also grateful to my family and friends for so much enthusiasm and support around my art book series. Special thanks to Constance, Ann, Phyllis and Martin, Beverly, Terri and Brenda, Jay and Kim, the parents and teachers of my young students, all the Lipseys up in Michigan, my parents, my husband Martin, and the Great Creator.

Index